The Magic School Bus
Inside the Earth

The Magic School Bus
Inside the Earth

By Joanna Cole   Illustrated by Bruce Degen

SCHOLASTIC
HARDCOVER

SCHOLASTIC INC. / *New York*

The author and illustrator wish to thank Dr. George E. Harlow, Associate Curator,
Department of Mineral Sciences at The American Museum of Natural History,
for his assistance in preparing this book.

The author would also like to thank Dr. Peter Bower, Professor of Geology at Barnard College,
for his helpful consultation.

Library of Congress Cataloging-in-Publication
Cole, Joanna.
The magic school bus.
(Scholastic hardcover)
Summary: On a special field trip in the
magic school bus, Ms. Frizzle's class learns
at first hand about different kinds of rocks
and the formation of the earth.
1. Physical geology—Juvenile literature.
[1. Earth—Internal structure.   2. Geology]
I. Degen, Bruce, ill.   II. Title.
QE29.C696   1987   551   87-4563
ISBN 0-590-40759-7

12 11 10 9 8 7 6 5   0 1 2 3 4/9

Printed in the U.S.A.

FIRST SCHOLASTIC PRINTING, OCTOBER 1987

In Ms. Frizzle's class,
we had been learning about
animals' homes
for almost a month.
We were pretty tired of it.
So everyone was happy
when Ms. Frizzle announced,
"Today we start something new."

SOMETHING NEW.
THANK GOODNESS!

GET OFF!

Beaver Lodge

PRAIRIE DOG
TOWN

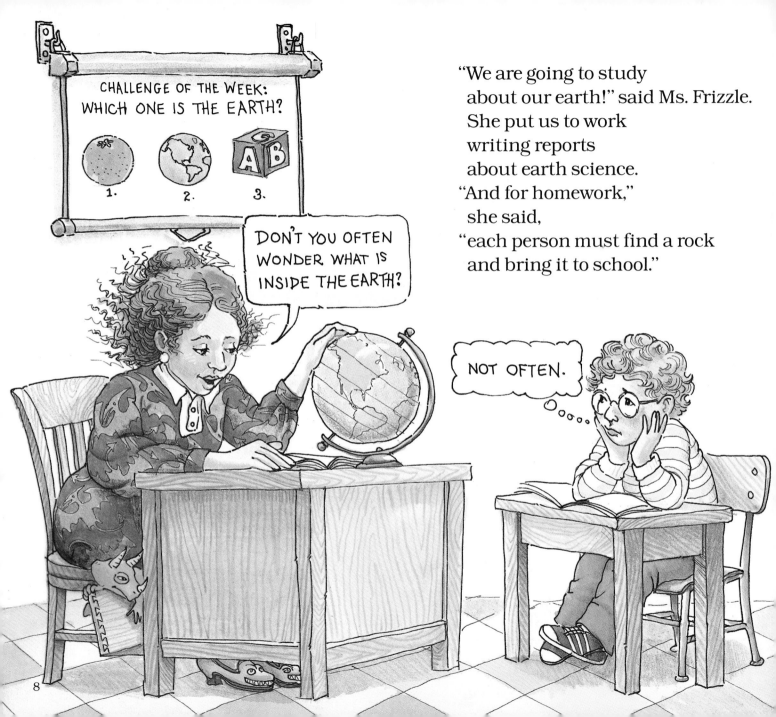

CHALLENGE OF THE WEEK:
WHICH ONE IS THE EARTH?

1.   2.   3.

DON'T YOU OFTEN WONDER WHAT IS INSIDE THE EARTH?

NOT OFTEN.

"We are going to study about our earth!" said Ms. Frizzle. She put us to work writing reports about earth science. "And for homework," she said, "each person must find a rock and bring it to school."

But the next day, almost everyone had some excuse.

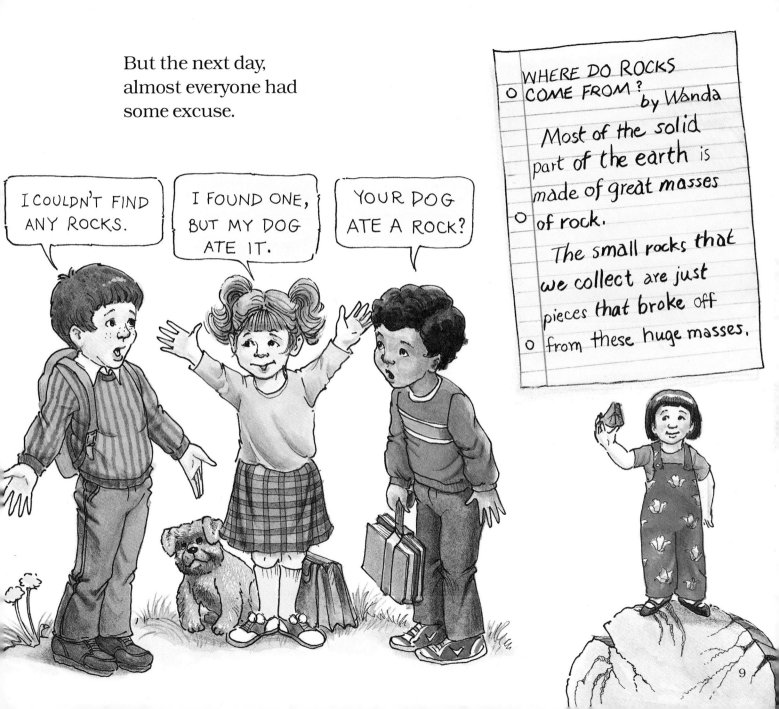

I COULDN'T FIND ANY ROCKS.

I FOUND ONE, BUT MY DOG ATE IT.

YOUR DOG ATE A ROCK?

WHERE DO ROCKS COME FROM? by Wanda

Most of the solid part of the earth is made of great masses of rock.

The small rocks that we collect are just pieces that broke off from these huge masses.

9

Only four people
had done the homework.
And Phil was the only one
who had found a real rock.

THAT'S NOT A ROCK!

IT IS _TOO_ A ROCK!

IT'S PART OF AN OLD **7-UP** BOTTLE.

YOU CHIPPED THIS OFF THE SIDEWALK, DIDN'T YOU, WANDA?

MY ROCK
ALEX

MY ROCK
QUARTZITE
PHIL

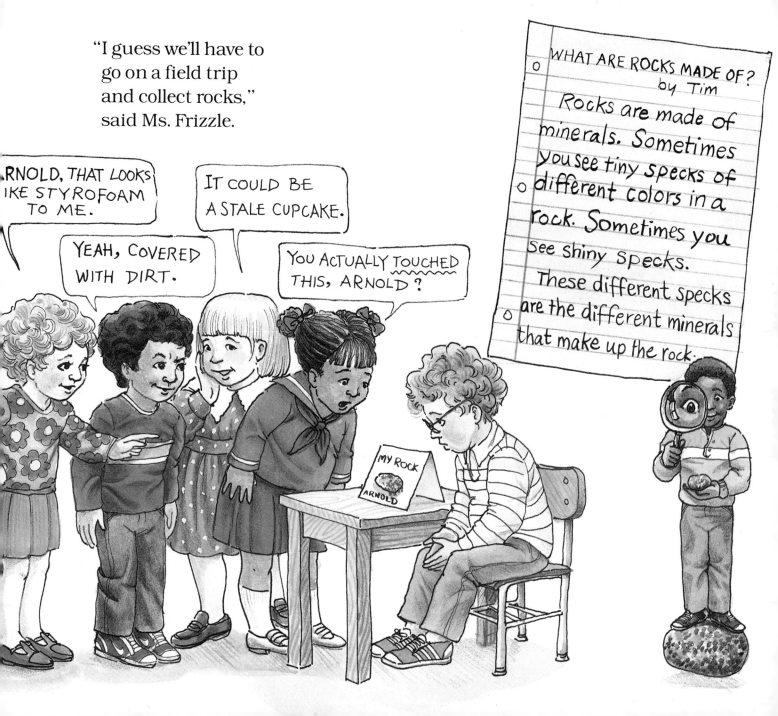

You never know
what will happen
on a trip with Ms. Frizzle.
Her new dress
was a trip in itself.
At first the old school bus
wouldn't start.
But finally we were on our way.

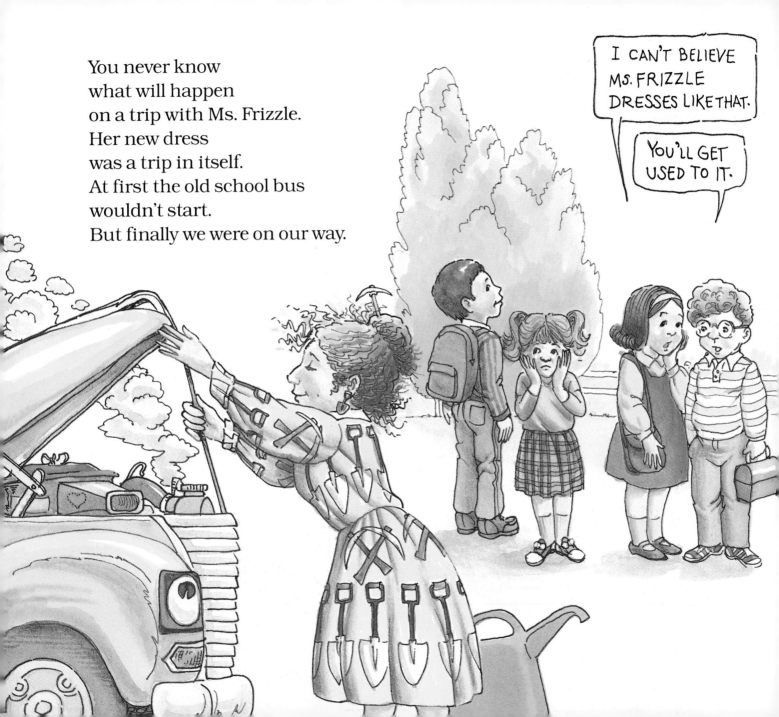

I CAN'T BELIEVE MS. FRIZZLE DRESSES LIKE THAT.

YOU'LL GET USED TO IT.

When we came to the field,
all the kids wanted
to get out of the bus.
But suddenly,
the bus began to spin like a top.
That sort of thing doesn't happen
on most class trips.

13

THE EARTH'S CRUST
by John

The outside of the earth is a shell of hard rock and soil. This shell is called the earth's crust.

When the spinning finally stopped,
some things had changed.
We all had on new clothes.
The bus had turned into
a steam shovel.
And there were shovels and picks
for every kid in the class.
"Start digging!"
yelled Ms. Frizzle.
And we began making a huge hole
right in the middle of the field.

THIS CRUST IS AS HARD AS A ROCK, TOO.

THIS ISN'T EXACTLY EASY.

AT LEAST WE'RE MISSING SPELLING.

DIG IT!

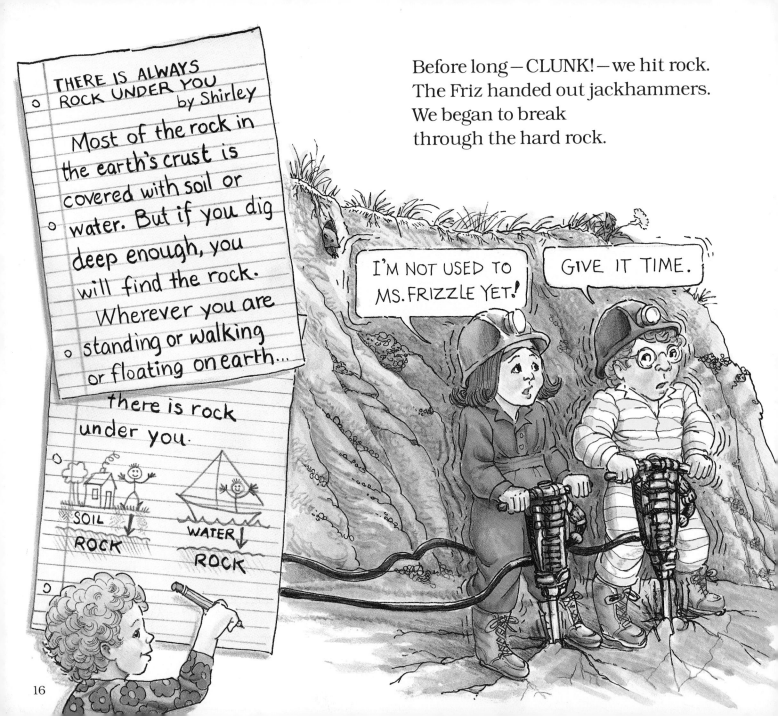

THERE IS ALWAYS
ROCK UNDER YOU
by Shirley

Most of the rock in the earth's crust is covered with soil or water. But if you dig deep enough, you will find the rock.

Wherever you are standing or walking or floating on earth...

there is rock under you.

SOIL
ROCK

WATER
ROCK

Before long—CLUNK!—we hit rock.
The Friz handed out jackhammers.
We began to break
through the hard rock.

I'M NOT USED TO MS. FRIZZLE YET!

GIVE IT TIME.

16

"Hey, these rocks have stripes," said a kid.
Ms. Frizzle explained that each stripe was a different kind of rock.

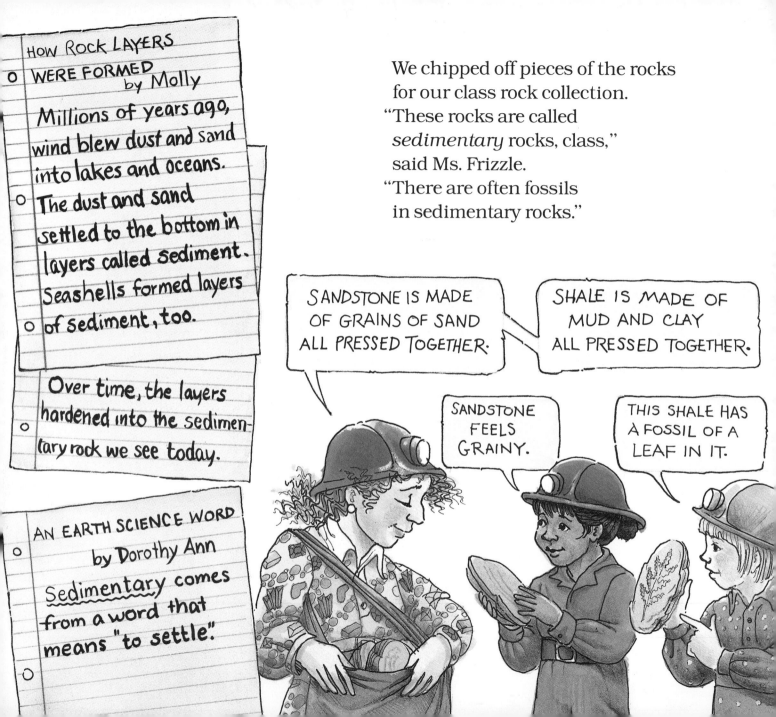

HOW ROCK LAYERS
WERE FORMED
by Molly

Millions of years ago, wind blew dust and sand into lakes and oceans. The dust and sand settled to the bottom in layers called sediment. Seashells formed layers of sediment, too.

Over time, the layers hardened into the sedimentary rock we see today.

AN EARTH SCIENCE WORD
by Dorothy Ann

Sedimentary comes from a word that means "to settle."

We chipped off pieces of the rocks for our class rock collection. "These rocks are called *sedimentary* rocks, class," said Ms. Frizzle. "There are often fossils in sedimentary rocks."

SANDSTONE IS MADE OF GRAINS OF SAND ALL PRESSED TOGETHER.

SHALE IS MADE OF MUD AND CLAY ALL PRESSED TOGETHER.

SANDSTONE FEELS GRAINY.

THIS SHALE HAS A FOSSIL OF A LEAF IN IT.

Wouldn't you know it?
Just when we were finding
lots of fossils,
Ms. Frizzle said,
"Back on the bus, kids."
Then, as we were driving along,
we heard rock crumbling underneath u
Down we went.
Everything was pitch black.
And we were falling, falling, falling!

We landed with a bump.
Ms. Frizzle switched on the headlights.
We had fallen through a hole
into a huge limestone cave.
"Rain water has been dripping down
through the earth for ages,"
said Ms. Frizzle.
"The water wore away this cave
in the rock."

THIS WHOLE CAVE IS MADE OF LIMESTONE. CAN YOU FIND MORE FOSSILS HERE?

HERE'S ONE, MS. FRIZZLE.

KNOCK IT OFF!

THE EMPIRE STATE BUILDING IS MADE OF LIMESTONE, TOO.

We wanted to stay for a while,
but suddenly, the bus sprouted a drill.
It started boring through the rock.
Frizzie shouted, "Follow that bus!"
And down we went.

LOOK! A STALAGMITE GROWING FROM THE GROUND...

AND A STALACTITE HANGING FROM THE CEILING!

How STALAGMITES AND STALACTITES ARE FORMED
by Phil

Shapes that look like cones and icicles are formed in caves by dripping water that contains tiny invisible bits of limestone.

HOW TO REMEMBER WHICH IS WHICH:
The word stalagmite has a '**g**' for ground.
The word stalactite has a '**c**' for ceiling.

The farther down we went,
the hotter it got.
The rocks were harder, too.
"These are rocks that were changed
from one kind to another kind
by heat and pressure,"
explained The Friz.
"Rocks that were changed
are called *metamorphic* rocks."

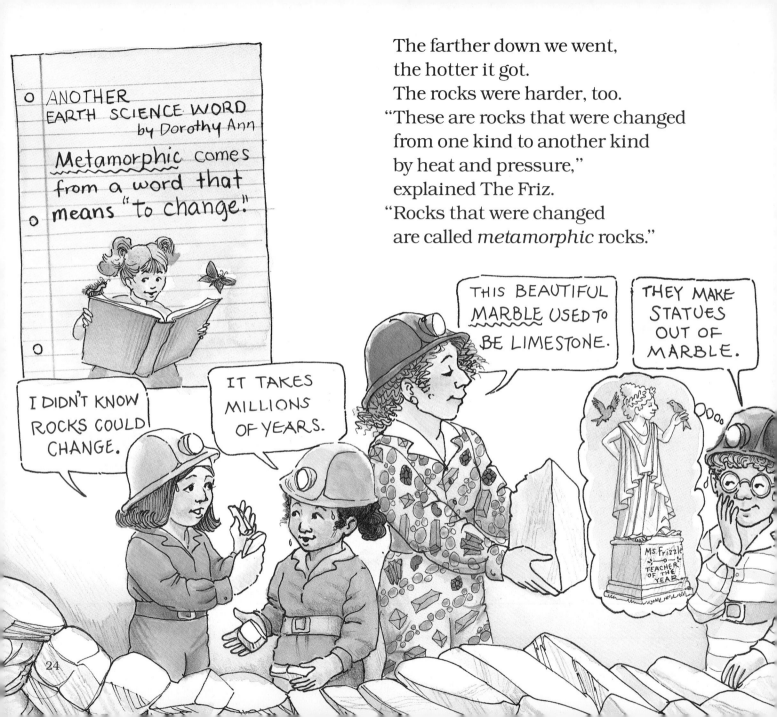

ANOTHER
EARTH SCIENCE WORD
by Dorothy Ann

Metamorphic comes
from a word that
means "to change."

I DIDN'T KNOW ROCKS COULD CHANGE.

IT TAKES MILLIONS OF YEARS.

THIS BEAUTIFUL MARBLE USED TO BE LIMESTONE.

THEY MAKE STATUES OUT OF MARBLE.

MS. Frizzle
TEACHER OF THE YEAR

24

We had dug all the way
through the earth's crust.
It was so hot now
that Ms. Frizzle told us to
get back in the bus.

She stepped on the gas,
and the bus started *really* drilling.
Soon we were actually inside the earth.
It was hot, hot, hot!
And it got hotter and hotter
as we zoomed toward the center.

We were glad when Ms. Frizzle
headed out again.
We reached the earth's crust
and drove straight up through
a tunnel of black rock.
It was great to see the sky.

WHAT IS INSIDE THE EARTH
by Ralph

Under the earth's crust
there are pockets of
melted rock. Below this
is the **mantle**, made of
solid hot rock.

The **outer core** is
liquid metal and the
very center of the
earth, the **inner core**,
is a ball of solid metal
larger than the moon!

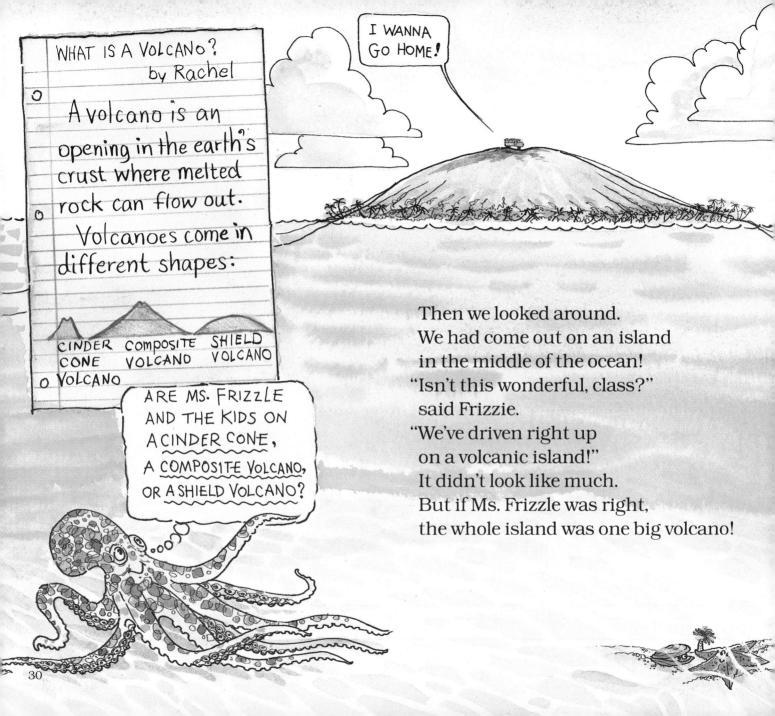

Then we looked around.
We had come out on an island
in the middle of the ocean!
"Isn't this wonderful, class?"
said Frizzie.
"We've driven right up
on a volcanic island!"
It didn't look like much.
But if Ms. Frizzle was right,
the whole island was one big volcano!

We were nervous, but Ms. Frizzle made us collect some rocks.
She said they had all hardened from melted rock that had come out of the volcano.
Then, suddenly, we heard rumblings from below.

HE BLACK ROCK 'RE WALKING ON S BASALT.

HIS SHINY OLCANIC GLASS S OBSIDIAN.

HEY! THIS ROCK FLOATS!

THAT'S PUMICE. AIR BUBBLES INSIDE MAKE IT THE LIGHTEST ROCK THERE IS.

I HEAR RUMBLING!

IS THAT YOUR STOMACH, ARNOLD?

VOLCANOES MAKE NEW LAND by Arnold

The material that comes out of a volcano is melted rock called <u>lava</u>. When lava cools, it hardens into new rock. In time, soil forms on the rock and plants can grow.

I DIDN'T KNOW VOLCANOES COULD BE USEFUL!

We scrambled into the bus.
The Friz turned the ignition key and stepped on the gas.
Nothing happened.
The bus would not start!
We thought we were goners!

UH-OH

Red-hot lava came streaming
out of the volcano.
Some of it shot into the air
like a fountain.
Some of it flowed over the land
like a river.
Our bus went along with it—
right into the sea.

CLASS, WHEN THIS LAVA HARDENS,
IT WILL BE THE <u>NEWEST</u> ROCK
ON EARTH.

WHO CARES?
JUST GET US
OUT OF HERE!

SSSSS

HISSSSS

HISSSSSSSS

When the red-hot lava hit the water,
it made a huge cloud of steam.
All we could see was white.
We seemed to be rising
with the steam and floating along.
No one knows how long
we floated in the cloud...

WHERE ARE WE?

I DON'T KNOW,
BUT I HAVE TO BE
HOME BY 3:30.

but when it finally cleared,
we were back in the school parking lot.

It had been a weird trip,
but we *did* get
a great rock collection
for our classroom.

A WORD WITH THE AUTHOR AND THE ARTIST

The first reader of this book called to complain. He said the book was full of mistakes. We recorded the conversation to help you decide which things are true and which were put in to make the story more exciting.

READER: This book is full of mistakes!

AUTHOR: It is not!

ARTIST: Everything in this book is absolutely true and really happened.

READER: What about the beaver lodge on page 7?

AUTHOR: Oh, that. Well, I guess that *would* be too messy in a real classroom.

READER: And the beehive?

ARTIST: That, too. But everything else is fact.

READER: Oh, come *on!* You mean kids can use jackhammers (page 16), and a bus can change into a steam shovel (page 14) and a drill (page 23)?

AUTHOR: Well, er, now that you mention it, that is not really possible.

READER: And do you expect me to believe that a bus can go through the center of the earth (page 28)?

ARTIST: Yes....

AUTHOR: Maybe....

ARTIST: Well, actually, no. The bus couldn't do that, either.

AUTHOR: Even if a bus *could* drill its way through, the distance is so long that the trip would take months, even years.

READER: And what about the heat?

AUTHOR: Okay, okay! It's white-hot in the center of the earth. The bus would be burned up in a minute.

READER: Isn't it kind of ridiculous to say that air-conditioning would help?

AUTHOR: Gee, you're a tough cookie! Okay, you're right. Air-conditioning could not make any difference in that kind of heat.

READER: And the bus could not flow in lava and go up in a cloud of steam (pages 33-34)?

ARTIST: Give us a break! You're right again. That's not true, either.

READER: But you said *everything* was true!

AUTHOR: Everything *else* is. Honest!

READER: Everything else is true? There truly are sedimentary, metamorphic, and igneous rocks?

AUTHOR: Certainly!

READER: And lava really does harden into new rock?

ARTIST: Oh, yes.

READER: And what about Ms. Frizzle's clothing?

AUTHOR: That *is* hard to believe, but it's true.

ARTIST: She really does dress that way!

HOW TO SAY OUR NEW EARTH SCIENCE WORDS

basalt
(buh·SAWLT)

granite
(GRAN·it)

igneous
(IHG·nee·uhs)

lava
(LAH·vuh)

metamorphic
(met·uh·MAWR·fik)

obsidian
(ahb·SIHD·ee·un)

pumice
(PUHM·ihs)

quartzite
(KWAWRT·site)

sedimentary
(sed·uh·MEN·tar·ee)

stalactite
(stuh·LAK·tite)

stalagmite
(stuh·LAG·mite)